Module B4 — The Processes of Life

Module B4 — The Processes of Life

Page 1 — Cell Structure and Function

Q1 Enzymes for aerobic respiration are found in mitochondria.
Enzymes for anaerobic respiration are found in the cytoplasm.
Enzymes for photosynthesis are found in chloroplasts.

Q2 a) aerobic, mitochondria
b) cell membrane
c) proteins, cytoplasm

Q3 nucleus, proteins, enzymes, chlorophyll

Q4

	Animal cell	Yeast cell	Bacterial cell
Nucleus	✔	✔	
Cytoplasm	✔	✔	✔
Cell membrane	✔	✔	✔
Cell wall		✔	✔
Mitochondria	✔	✔	
Circular DNA molecule			✔

Pages 2-3 — Enzymes

Q1 a) Enzymes are proteins that speed up chemical reactions.
b) instructions
c) the active site
d)

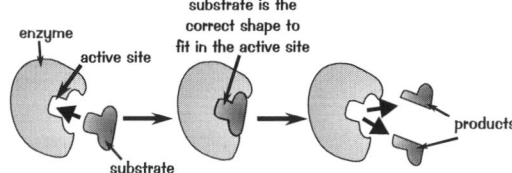

enzyme
active site
substrate is the correct shape to fit in the active site
substrate
products

Q2 a) 35 °C (one degree either way acceptable)
b) The rate of reaction increased with increasing temperature up to the enzyme's optimum temperature.
c) At 45°C the enzyme is denatured. At this temperature some of the bonds holding the enzyme together break. This changes the shape of the enzyme's active site.

Q3 a)

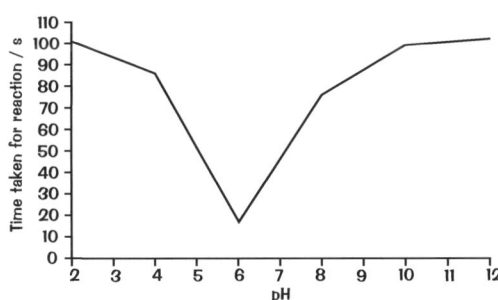

b) about pH 6
c) If the pH is too high or too low, it interferes with the bonds holding the enzymes together. This changes the shape of the active site and denatures the enzyme.
d) No. This enzyme works very slowly at low pHs.

Page 4 — Aerobic Respiration

Q1 a) True
b) False
c) True
d) True
e) False
f) False

Q2 word: glucose + oxygen → carbon dioxide + water (+ energy)
symbol: $C_6H_{12}O_6 + 6O_2 \rightarrow 6CO_2 + 6H_2O$ (+ energy)

Q3 a) E.g. In plant cells, glucose is joined together to make things like starch and cellulose. / In plant cells, animal cells and microorganisms, glucose and nitrates are joined together to make amino acids, which are then joined together to make proteins.
b) E.g. movement, active transport

Page 5 — Anaerobic Respiration

Q1 a) little or no
b) waterlogged
c) under
d) vigorous

Q2 a) i) glucose → ethanol + carbon dioxide (+ energy)
ii) glucose → lactic acid (+ energy)
b) ethanol, carbon dioxide

Q3 a) Microorganisms ferment plant and animal waste that contains carbohydrates to produce biogas.
b) Yeast ferment the carbohydrates in flour and release carbon dioxide — this causes bread to rise.
c) Yeast ferment sugar to form alcohol/ethanol.

Page 6 — Photosynthesis

Q1 a) It's a series of chemical reactions that uses energy from sunlight to produce food.
b) carbon dioxide + water → glucose + oxygen
c) $6CO_2 + 6H_2O \rightarrow C_6H_{12}O_6 + 6O_2$
d) chlorophyll — a green substance needed for photosynthesis
oxygen — a waste product of photosynthesis
sunlight — supplies the energy for photosynthesis
glucose — the food that is produced by photosynthesis

Q2 energy, starch, cellulose/chlorophyll, chlorophyll/cellulose, nitrogen, soil

Q3 They make energy from the Sun available to other organisms by converting it into glucose. The energy is transferred when the photosynthetic organisms are eaten.

Pages 7-8 — Rate of Photosynthesis

Q1 It's something which stops photosynthesis from happening any faster.

Q2 a) Increasing the concentration of CO_2 increases the rate of photosynthesis up to a certain point.
b) The rate of photosynthesis doesn't continue to increase because something else (e.g. temperature) becomes the limiting factor.

Q3 a)

b) The rate of photosynthesis increased as the light intensity increased.
c) The relationship would continue up to a point, and then the graph would level off. At this point, either the temperature or amount of carbon dioxide would become a limiting factor.

Q4 a) 00.00 (midnight)
b) There's no light at night so photosynthesis won't occur.

Module B5 — Growth and Development

c)

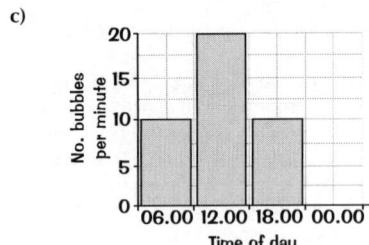

Q5 a)

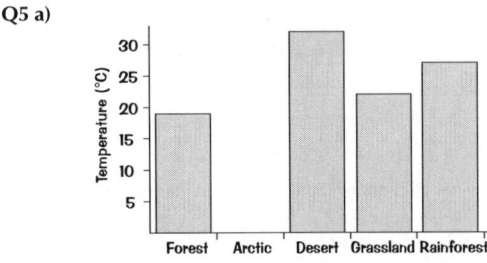

b) In the Arctic.

c) The temperatures are low there, so the rate of photosynthesis will be slow because the enzymes needed for photosynthesis will be working slowly.

Q6 a) E.g. temperature

b) The faster the rate of photosynthesis, the faster the growth rate of the grass.

Page 9 — Investigating Photosynthesis

Q1 a) E.g. a light meter

b) i) It's a square frame (divided into a grid of 100 smaller squares).

ii) You place the quadrat on the ground and then count the number of squares in the quadrat that are more than half-covered by the plant species.

c) i) To investigate how something changes across an area.

ii) 1. Run a tape measure between two fixed points.
2. Start at one end of the tape measure and collect your data.
3. Move along the tape measure and collect your data again.
4. Keep moving along the tape measure and collecting your data until the other end is reached.

d) Flowering plant (it has seeds and flowers).

Page 10 — Diffusion, Osmosis and Active Transport

Q1 passive, higher, lower, carbon dioxide and oxygen

Q2 a) B

b) The liquid level on side B will fall, because there will be an overall movement of water molecules from side B, which is more dilute/has a higher concentration of water molecules, to side A, which is more concentrated/has a lower concentration of water molecules.

Q3 a) The overall moment of chemicals across a cell membrane using energy released by respiration (from a region of lower concentration to a region of higher concentration).

b) E.g. Plants take in minerals like nitrates through their roots.

Pages 11-12 — Mixed Questions — Module B4

Q1 glucose + oxygen → carbon dioxide + water (+ energy)

Q2 a) Diffusion — the passive overall movement of particles from a region of their higher concentration to a region of their lower concentration.
Osmosis — the overall movement of water from a dilute to a more concentrated solution through a partially permeable membrane.

b) plant roots take in water by osmosis

Q3 a) i) oxygen

ii) carbon dioxide, water

b) E.g. for respiration, to make chemicals for growth, for storing as starch.

c) E.g. phytoplankton

Q4 a) amount of light, amount of carbon dioxide

b) E.g. temperature

c) E.g. a heater

Q5 a) i) False

ii) True

iii) True

iv) False

v) False

b) E.g. All enzymes are proteins.
E.g. A denatured enzyme is one that won't work any more because the shape of the active site has changed.
E.g. Most enzymes only speed up one specific reaction.

c) i) mitochondria

ii) chloroplasts

Module B5 — Growth and Development

Page 13 — DNA — Making Proteins

Q1 a) a double helix

b) four

c) Adenine (A) always pairs with thymine (T), and cytosine (C) with guanine (G).

Q2 a) True

b) False

c) False

d) True

e) True

f) False

Q3 a) i)

ii) Eight (there are eight groups of three bases).

b) 2, 3, 1, 4, 4, 3, 1, 1

Page 14 — Cell Division — Mitosis

Q1 two, genetically, parent, copies, growth, damaged

Q2 a) true

b) false

c) true

Q3 a) The two arms of each chromosome are separated.

b) Membranes form around each of the sets of chromosomes, becoming the nuclei of the two new cells.

c) The cytoplasm divides to form two new cells.

CGP

GCSE

Additional Science

Exam Board: OCR 21st Century

Answer Book

Higher Level

Contents

Published by CGP

ISBN: 978 1 84762 749 0

Groovy website: www.cgpbooks.co.uk

Printed by Elanders Ltd, Newcastle upon Tyne.
Jolly bits of clipart from CorelDRAW®

Based on the classic CGP style created by Richard Parsons.

Module B5 — Growth and Development

Page 15 — Cell Division — Meiosis

Q1 a) Meiosis
b) Mitosis, Meiosis
c) Meiosis
d) Meiosis

Q2

	What is it?	Number of Chromosomes	Formed by
A	egg cell	23	meiosis
B	sperm cell	23	meiosis
C	fertilised egg cell	46	fertilisation

Q3 a) Sperm and egg cells that only have one copy of each chromosome.
b) So that when two gametes join together during fertilisation the resulting zygote will have the full number of chromosomes.

Page 16 — Animal Development

Q1 mitosis, embryo, stem cells, specialised, eight, tissues
Q2 1. Take an egg cell.
2. Remove the genetic material.
3. Insert the nucleus from a body cell of an adult you want to clone.
4. The inactive genes in the body cell's nucleus are switched on under the right conditions.
5. An embryo forms.
6. Extract embryonic stem cells.
Q3 They're used to produce cells to replace damaged tissues.
Q4 Embryonic stem cells can differentiate into any type of specialised cell. Adult stem cells can become specialised but they aren't as versatile — they can only turn into certain types of cell.

Page 17 — Plant Development

Q1 a) meristems
b) i) true
ii) false
iii) true
c) E.g. xylem, phloem
Q2 a) Parts of plant that have been cut off to make new plants.
b) E.g. auxins
c)

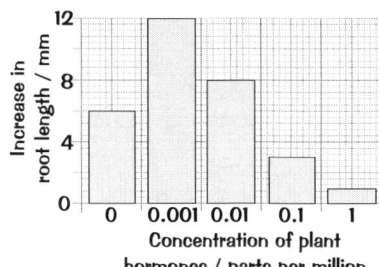

d) 0.001 parts per million

Page 18 — Phototropism and Auxins

Q1 a) Positive phototropism is growth towards a light source.
Negative phototropism is growth away from a light source.

b) Positive phototropism: plants need sunlight for photosynthesis to produce food for energy and growth. Photosynthesis occurs mainly in the leaves, so plant shoots need to grow towards the light so that the plant can survive.
Negative phototropism: plants need water and nutrients from the soil to grow, so plant roots need to grow down into the soil to absorb them so the plant can survive.

Q2 a) the tip
b) auxins
c)

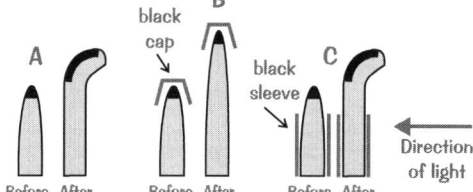

Q3 a) i) the shoot will grow towards the right
ii) the shoot will grow straight up
b) i) The auxins soak into the cells on the left-hand side of the shoot, making these cells elongate faster than those on the right. This causes the shoot to grow towards the right.
ii) The auxins soak into all the cells at the top of the cut shoot, making all the cells elongate at the same rate. The shoot grows straight upwards.

Pages 19-20 — Mixed Questions — Module B5

Q1 Mitosis is where cell division produces two new cells that are identical to each other and the parent cell.
Meiosis is where cell division produces gametes.

Q2

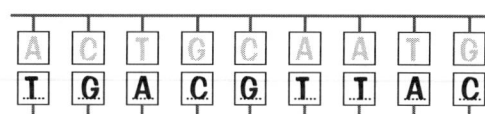

Q3 1. The DNA strand unzips.
2. A molecule of messenger RNA is made using DNA as a template.
3. Messenger RNA moves out of the nucleus.
4. Messenger RNA joins with an organelle that makes proteins.
5. Amino acids are joined together to make a protein.
Q4 a) Meristems produce unspecialised cells that are able to divide and form any cell type, so a cutting with meristems can grow into a new plant.
b) i) clone
ii) desirable features
c) Rooting powder contains plant hormones/auxins that makes cuttings produce roots rapidly.
Q5 a) phototropism
b) i) False
ii) False
iii) False
iv) True
c) Plant shoots grow towards light.
Plant roots grow away from light.
Negative phototropism ensures that roots grow deep into the soil for nutrients.
Q6 a) i) a group of specialised cells
ii) a group of tissues
b) E.g. because the embryos used to provide the stem cells are destroyed and they could have become a person.
c) All of, the same, off, proteins, stem, on, type

Module B6 — Brain and Mind

Module B6 — Brain and Mind

Pages 21-22 — The Nervous System

Q1 change, environment, receptors, nervous, hormonal, multicellular

Q2 a) central nervous system

b) The CNS coordinates responses to stimuli.

c)

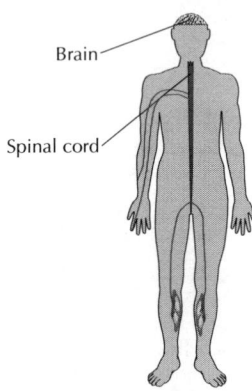

Brain

Spinal cord

d) The peripheral nervous system connects the CNS to the rest of the body.

e) i) sensory neurones

ii) motor neurones

Q3

Q4 a) Effectors respond to nerve impulses and bring about changes.

b) Receptors are cells that detect stimuli.

c)

	Example	Make up part of...
Receptor	taste buds	the tongue
	light receptor cells	the eye
Effector	muscle cells	muscles
	hormone secreting cells	glands

Q5 1. Temperature receptors in Jamie's hand detect the increase in temperature.
2. Impulses travel along a sensory neurone.
3. The information is processed by the spinal cord.
4. Impulses travel along a motor neurone.
5. Some of the muscles in Jamie's hand contract, causing him to drop the pan.

Pages 23-24 — Neurones and Synapses

Q1 a) As electrical impulses.

b) axon, cytoplasm, membrane

c) Fatty sheath — it insulates the neurone from neighbouring cells and increases the speed of transmission of a nerve impulse.

Q2 a) synapse

b) As an impulse reaches the end of a neurone it triggers the release of transmitter chemicals into the synapse. The chemicals diffuse across the synapse and bind to receptor molecules on the membrane of the next neurone.

Q3 E.g. Ecstasy blocks the sites in the brain where the transmitter chemical serotonin is removed. Because it can't be removed, the serotonin concentration increases, which affects a person's mood.

Q4 chemical, oestrogen, blood, slow, neurones, effector, electrical, fast

Q5 a) Serotonin is a transmitter chemical and only specific transmitter chemicals can bind to the receptor molecules on neurones to trigger impulses.

b) e.g. MDMA/ecstasy

c) e.g. beta blockers

Page 25 — Reflexes

Q1 a) quickly

b) spinal cord, an unconscious

c) involuntary

d) arc

e) the same

Q2 E.g. stepping / grasping / sucking/suckling

Q3 a) False

b) True

c) True

d) False

Q4 stimulus, receptors, sensory, relay, CNS, motor, effector

Page 26 — Modifying and Learning Reflexes

Q1 a) i) The smell of food.

ii) The bell ringing.

iii) Salivating in response to the smell of food.

iv) Salivating in response to the sound of a bell.

b) The conditioned reflex has been learnt.

c) no direct connection

Q2 a) 1. A bird spots a red coloured caterpillar. It swoops down, catches and eats the caterpillar.
2. The bird feels unwell because of poisons in the insect.
3. The bird learns to associate feeling unwell with the red colour.
4. The bird spots a red coloured caterpillar and avoids it.
5. The bird increases its chances of survival by avoiding the caterpillar and being poisoned.

b) Feeling unwell.

Q3 E.g. the modification of a reflex to keep hold of a hot plate of food. The reflex is modified via a neurone (from the brain) to the motor neurone of the reflex arc.

Page 27 — Brain Development and Learning

Q1 a) False

b) True

c) True

d) False

Q2 formed, developed, experience, more, stimulated, unconnected, network, trillions

Q3 When experiences are repeated over and over again the pathways that they travel down become strengthened. Strengthened pathways are more likely to transmit nerve impulses than others.

Page 28 — Learning Skills and Behaviour

Q1 Complex animals have a huge number/trillions of potential pathways in the brain. This makes them more adaptable than simple animals without brains.

Q2 a) The ability to talk depends on a child hearing other people speak and Isabelle hadn't had this experience.

Module C4 — Chemical Patterns

b) Children must learn to speak before they reach a certain age, e.g. around eleven years old, or they never will. Isabelle was found when she was six and she learnt how to speak, but Tissa was eleven when he was found and he never learnt how to speak.

Q3 a) the cerebral cortex
b) E.g. intelligence / consciousness

Page 29 — Studying the Brain

Q1 E.g. studying patients with brain damage / electrically stimulating the brain / MRI scans.
Q2 It's the storage and retrieval of information.
Q3 a) Number B — there is a pattern in the number and humans are better able to remember information if they can see (or impose) a pattern on the information.
b) E.g. any three from: smell, colour, light, sound.
c) E.g. repetition of information.
Q4 a)

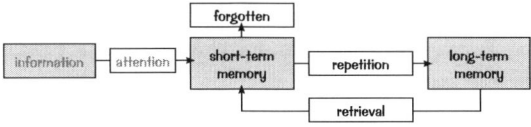

b) false

Pages 30-31 — Mixed Questions
— Module B6

Q1 a) A change in the environment of an organism.
b) receptors
c) effectors
d) The PNS is made up of sensory and motor neurones and it connects the central nervous system/CNS to the rest of the body.
Q2 a) E.g. any two from: knee jerk reflex, pupil reflex, dropping a hot object
b) 1. A stimulus is detected by receptor cells.
2. An impulse is sent along a sensory neurone to the CNS.
3. The impulse is passed along a relay neurone.
4. The impulse is sent along a motor neurone.
5. The impulse reaches an effector, which reacts to the stimulus.
c) Reflexes need to happen fast so electrical nerve impulses are used for them because they travel round the body quicker than hormones.
Q3 a) i) axon
ii) synapse
iii) fatty sheath
b) E.g. It acts as an electrical insulator, shielding the neurone from neighbouring cells and speeding up the transmission of the electrical impulse.
Q4 repeated, strengthened, more, practised, harder
Q5 a) The reflex response can be overridden by a neurone that runs between the brain and the motor neurone of his reflex arc.
b) It prevents Stephen from dropping his cup of tea.

Module C4 — Chemical Patterns

Page 32 — Atoms

Q1

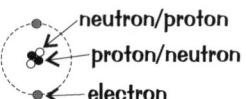

neutron/proton
proton/neutron
electron

Q2

Particle	Mass	Charge
Proton	1	+1
Neutron	**1**	0
Electron	0.0005	−1

Q3 a) 0
b) shells
c) protons, electrons (in either order)
d) protons
e) nucleus

Q4)

element	electrons	protons
magnesium	12	**12**
carbon	**6**	6
oxygen	**8**	**8**

Pages 33-34 — Chemical Equations

Q1 a) Correctly balanced
b) Incorrectly balanced
c) Incorrectly balanced
d) Correctly balanced
e) Correctly balanced
Q2 $2C + O_2 \rightarrow 2CO$
Q3 a) Reactants: sodium and water
Products: sodium hydroxide and hydrogen
b) sodium + water → sodium hydroxide + hydrogen
c) $2Na + 2H_2O \rightarrow 2NaOH + H_2$
d) i) (l)
ii) (g)
Q4 a) $2Na + Cl_2 \rightarrow 2NaCl$
b) $4Li + O_2 \rightarrow 2Li_2O$
c) $MgCO_3 + 2HCl \rightarrow MgCl_2 + H_2O + CO_2$
d) $2Li + 2H_2O \rightarrow 2LiOH + H_2$
Q5 a) $CuO + \mathbf{2}HBr \rightarrow CuBr_2 + H_2O$
b) $H_2 + Br_2 \rightarrow \mathbf{2}HBr$
c) $\mathbf{2}Mg + O_2 \rightarrow 2MgO$
d) $2NaOH + H_2SO_4 \rightarrow Na_2SO_4 + \mathbf{2}H_2O$
Q6 a) $\mathbf{3}NaOH + AlBr_3 \rightarrow \mathbf{3}NaBr + Al(OH)_3$
b) $\mathbf{2}FeCl_2 + Cl_2 \rightarrow \mathbf{2}FeCl_3$
c) $N_2 + \mathbf{3}H_2 \rightarrow \mathbf{2}NH_3$
d) $\mathbf{4}Fe + 3O_2 \rightarrow 2Fe_2O_3$
e) $4NH_3 + 5O_2 \rightarrow 4NO + \mathbf{6}H_2O$

Page 35 — Line Spectrums

Q1 a) colours, heated
b) potassium
Q2 a) electrons, excited, light, light, line, elements, light, electron, element, line
b) They have been used to discover new elements.
Q3 Spectroscopy

Page 36 — History of the Periodic Table

Q1 a) true
b) false
c) true
d) false
Q2 E.g. He chose them based on their properties.
Q3 a) 1
b) Because he noticed that every eighth element had similar properties.
c) They hadn't been discovered when Newlands came up with his table.
Q4 a) germanium, 5.32 g/cm^3
b) i) Mendeleev arranged the elements in order of atomic mass and kept elements with similar properties in the same vertical groups, like Newlands.
ii) Unlike Newlands, Mendeleev left gaps for undiscovered elements.

Module C4 — Chemical Patterns

Pages 37-38 — The Modern Periodic Table

Q1 a) Any one of: sodium, magnesium, aluminium, phosphorus, sulfur, chlorine, argon.
b) Any one of: lithium, sodium, rubidium, caesium, francium.
c) Any one of: fluorine, chlorine, bromine, iodine, astatine.
d) Any one of: lithium, sodium, potassium, rubidium, caesium, francium.

Q2

Name	Symbol	Relative atomic mass	Proton number
Iron	Fe	56	**26**
Lead	Pb	207	**82**
Xenon	**Xe**	**131**	54
Copper	**Cu**	**63.5**	29

Q3 a) radon and krypton
b) silicon and sodium
c) nickel
d) silicon/iodine
Q4 a) vertical
b) group
c) increasing
d) right-hand
e) similar
Q5 a) True
b) True
c) False
d) True
e) True
Q6 Any two of: helium, neon, krypton, xenon and radon.

Q7

Element	Relative atomic mass	Number of protons	Number of electrons	Number of neutrons
Potassium	39	**19**	19	**20**
Phosphorous	31	15	**15**	**16**
Neon	**20**	10	**10**	10

Q8 a) The following should be ticked: A and D
b) Boron: **non-metal**
Aluminium: **metal**

Page 39 — Electron Shells

Q1 a) i) True
ii) False
iii) True
iv) False
v) True
vi) True
b) ii) E.g. the lowest energy levels are always filled first.
iv) E.g. reactive elements have partially filled outer shells.
Q2 E.g. the innermost electron shell should be filled first / there should be two electrons in the inner shell. / The outer shell contains too many electrons (it only holds a maximum of 8 electrons).
Q3 a) 2, 2
b) 2, 6
c) 2, 8, 4
d) 2, 8, 8, 2
e) 2, 8, 3
f) 2, 8, 8
Q4 a) 2, 8, 7
b)
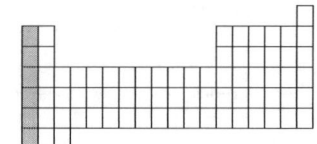

Page 40 — Ionic Bonding

Q1 a) electrons, ions
b) charged particles
c) attracted to
Q2 a) one
b) +1
c) NaCl
Q3 a) True
b) False
c) True
d) True
e) False
f) True
Q4 The bromine atom gains one electron (so it has a full outer shell) to become a –1 ion. It picks up this electron from the potassium.

Page 41 — Ions and Formulas

Q1 E.g. BeI_2, BeS, KI, K_2S
Q2 There are two chloride ions and one calcium ion (2^+). Each chloride ion must have a charge of **1$^-$**.
Q3 a) KBr
b) $FeSO_4$
c) CaF_2
Q4 a) Al_2O_3
b) 2^+
c) 1^-

Pages 42-43 — Group 1 — The Alkali Metals

Q1 a)

b) (least) lithium (Li), sodium (Na), potassium (K) (most).
Q2 1 electron.
Q3 a) The sodium would be shiny if it was freshly cut.
b) The sodium would be dull and tarnished.
c) The sodium will have reacted with the oxygen in the moist air.
Q4 a) Lower — the melting point decreases going down the group.
b) i) increases
ii) decreases
Q5 a) 2KCl (s)
b) The product will be a colourless crystalline salt.
c) They have similar electronic structures (each has 1 outer shell electron).
Q6 one, sodium hydroxide, hydrogen
Q7 a) A vigorous reaction. The lithium moves around the surface and fizzes.
b) The solution would turn purple, because lithium hydroxide is formed, which is alkaline.
c) $2Li (s) + 2H_2O (l) \rightarrow 2LiOH (aq) + H_2 (g)$
d) i) sodium + water → sodium hydroxide + hydrogen
ii) More vigorous — sodium is more reactive as it's further down the group.

Pages 44-45 — Group 7 — The Halogens

Q1 Bromine — Br — orange liquid — quite reactive
Chlorine — Cl — green gas — very reactive
Fluorine — F — yellow gas — most reactive
Iodine — I — grey solid — least reactive
Q2 a) False
b) True
c) True
d) False
e) True

Module C5 — Chemicals of the Natural Environment

Q3 a) $FeBr_3$ / Iron Bromide
b) $2Fe_{(s)} + 3Br_{2(g)} \rightarrow 2FeBr_{3(s)}$
Q4 Increases down the group — the melting points of the halogens, the boiling points of the halogens.
Decreases down the group — the reactivity of the halogens.
Q5 a) sodium bromide
b) $2Na + Br_2 \rightarrow 2NaBr$
c) i) Faster, because iodine is less reactive than bromine.
ii) Slower, because chlorine is more reactive than bromine.
Q6 a) Bromine is more reactive than iodine so it displaces it from the potassium iodide solution. Bromine is less reactive than chlorine so it doesn't displace it from the potassium chloride solution.
b) $Br_2 + 2KI \rightarrow I_2 + 2KBr$
c) i) yes
ii) no

Page 46 — Laboratory Safety

Q1 a) oxidising
b) highly flammable
c) toxic
d) explosive
e) corrosive
Q2 a) The alkali metals can react very violently if they come into contact with water vapour in the air.
b) It should be thoroughly dried.
c) The solutions are very alkaline and so are corrosive.
Q3 a) The halogens have poisonous vapours.
b) Corrosive substances attack and destroy living tissue (and other substances).

Page 47 — Mixed Questions — Module C4

Q1 a) Number of protons — 11
Number of neutrons — 12
Number of electron — 11
b) i) Sodium chloride is a colourless crystalline salt.
ii) $2Na\ (s) + Cl_2\ (g) \rightarrow 2NaCl\ (s)$
c) i) A solid ionic compound is made up of a giant lattice of ions. Each lattice forms a single crystal.
ii) The sodium gives up its outer electron and becomes an Na^+ ion. The chlorine atom picks up the spare electron and becomes a Cl^- ion. The oppositely charged ions attract each other and form an ionic bond.
Q2 a) 2, 8, 7
b) Chlorine only needs 1 electron to gain a full outer shell so it's very reactive.
c) Halogen X is chlorine.

Module C5 — Chemicals of the Natural Environment

Page 48 — Chemicals in the Atmosphere

Q1

substance	element or compound?	formula	percentage in atmosphere
oxygen	element	O_2	21%
carbon dioxide	compound	CO_2	0.04%
argon	element	Ar	1%
nitrogen	element	N_2	78%

Q2 non-metallic, molecular, atoms, strong, weak
Q3 a) low — only a little bit of energy is needed to overcome the weak forces between the molecules.
b) don't conduct — there are no free charges.
c) gases and liquids — only a little bit of energy is needed to overcome the weak forces between the molecules.
Q4 a) gas
b) liquid
c) solid

Pages 49-50 — Covalent Bonding

Q1 a) True
b) False
c) True
Q2 a)

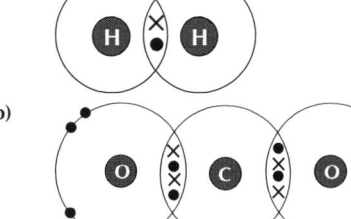

b)

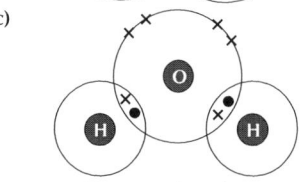

c)

Q3 positive, negative, electrostatic
Q4

DISPLAYED FORMULA		MOLECULAR FORMULA
H | H—C—H | H	a)	CH_4
H | N H H	b)	NH_3
O=S=O	c)	SO_2

Q5 a) It can't tell you anything about the 3-D shape of the molecule (e.g. the angle between the C–H bonds).
b)

Page 51 — Chemicals in the Hydrosphere

Q1 water, dissolved, ionic, salts, salty
Q2 a)

	When solid	When dissolved in water
Conducts electricity?	No	Yes

b) Potassium chloride is an ionic compound. When it is dissolved, the ions are free to move about and carry electric current. When it is solid the ions are held in place so it can't conduct electricity.
c) i) Na_2SO_4
ii) $MgCl_2$
iii) KBr
Q3 a) a regular, strong, positive, negative, large
b) Any two of, e.g. high boiling point, will dissolve to form solutions that conduct electricity, will conduct electricity when molten.

Module C5 — Chemicals of the Natural Environment

Page 52 — Identifying Positive Ions

Q1 In a flame test the different metal compounds will produce different colours when they are burnt.

Q2 a) Fe^{2+} (aq) + $2OH^-$ (aq) → $Fe(OH)_2$ (s)

b) Fe^{3+} (aq) + $3OH^-$ (aq) → $Fe(OH)_3$ (s)

c) Cilla would see a white precipitate at first, but it would redissolve in excess NaOH to form a colourless solution.

Q3 a) $CuSO_4$

b) $ZnSO_4$

c) $FeSO_4$

d) $FeCl_3$

Page 53 — Identifying Negative Ions

Q1 a) SO_4^{2-}

b) I^-

c) Br^-

Q2 acid, carbon dioxide, limewater

Q3 Solution 1 — bromide / Br^-

Solution 2 — sulfate, SO_4^{2-}

Solution 3 — carbonate / CO_3^{2-}

Q4 a) Ag^+ (aq) + **Cl^- (aq)** → AgCl (s)

b) 2HCl (aq) + Na_2CO_3 (s) → 2NaCl (aq) + **H_2O** (l) + **CO_2** (g)

c) **Ba^{2+} (aq) + SO_4^{2-} (aq)** → $BaSO_4$ (s)

Pages 54-55 — Chemicals in the Lithosphere

Q1 uncharged atoms, strong, high, insoluble

Q2 a) Each carbon atom in graphite forms three covalent bonds. Each has four outer electrons, so there are spare electrons not involved in bonds that are free to conduct electricity.

b) Each carbon atom in diamond forms four covalent bonds to give a very rigid structure held together very strongly. This makes it hard.

Q3 Sample A: sandstone
Reason: it contains a large percentage composition of silicon.
Sample B: limestone
Reason: it contains a large percentage composition of calcium.

Q4 crust, mantle, minerals, aluminium/silicon/oxygen, silicon/oxygen/aluminium, oxygen/aluminium/silicon.

Q5 a) Graphite — Use: pencils. Property: it is made of sheets of carbon atoms that can slide over each other. Layers can be rubbed off on to paper to give black pencil marks.

b) Diamond — Use: glass-cutting tool. Property: diamond is extremely hard (so it can cut through other substances).

Q6 a) silicon dioxide

b) silicon and oxygen

c) Any two from: e.g. high melting and boiling point — the strong covalent bonds between atoms are difficult to break and there are lots of them. / Doesn't conduct electricity — there are no free electrons to carry charge. / Hard — the atoms are bonded to each other by strong covalent bonds in a giant covalent structure that is hard to break.

Page 56 — Metals from Minerals

Q1 a) True

b) False

c) True

d) True

Q2 a) Carbon (in the wood) is more reactive than copper, so it can reduce the copper ore.

b) E.g. copper only makes up a small percentage of the ore so a lot needs to be mined.

Q3 carbon, below, oxidised, reduced, electrolysis, more

Q4 a) iron oxide + carbon → **iron** + **carbon dioxide**

b) **copper oxide + carbon** → copper + carbon dioxide

c) **Fe_2O_3(s)** + 3CO(g) → 2Fe(s) + 3CO_2(g)

d) 2ZnO(s) + **C(s)** → **2Zn(s)** + CO_2(g)

Pages 57-58 — Electrolysis

Q1 electric, dissolved/molten, molten/dissolved, decompose, electrolyte, taken from, external circuit, given to, molecules

Q2 A — (flow of) electrons
B — negative electrode / cathode
C — Al^{3+} / aluminium ion
D — (molten) aluminium
E — oxygen gas
F — O^{2-} / oxide ion
G — positive electrode / anode

Q3 For electricity to flow through the electrolyte, the ions need to be free to move. In a solid, the ions are in fixed positions. In a liquid or a solution they can move about.

Q4 a) i) True

ii) True

iii) False

iv) False

v) True

vi) True

b) iii) E.g During electrolysis, non-metals are attracted to the positive electrode.

iv) E.g. In the extraction of aluminium the electrolyte used is molten aluminium oxide.

Q5 a) aluminium oxide, Al_2O_3

b) Aluminium is more reactive than carbon (so the oxide will not be reduced by carbon).

Q6 a) The negative electrode.

b) Negative electrode: $Al^{3+} + 3e^- → Al$
Positive electrode: $2O^{2-} → O_2 + 4e^-$

Page 59 — Calculating Masses

Q1 a) mass, atom, carbon-12

b) i) 24

ii) 20

iii) 16

iv) 1

v) 12

vi) 63.5

vii) 39

viii) 40

ix) 35.5

Q2 a) You add the relative atomic masses of all the atoms in the compound together.

b) i) (2 × 1) + 16 = 18

ii) 39 + 16 + 1 = 56

iii) 1 + 14 + (3 × 16) = 63

iv) 24 + ((16 + 1) × 2) = 58

v) 56 + ((16 + 1)× 3) = 107

Q3 a) proportion of iron in iron oxide
= (A_r × number of atoms) ÷ M_r
= (56 × 2) ÷ 160 = 0.7
Mass = 0.7 × 500 g = 350 g

b) proportion of copper in copper oxide
= (A_r × number of atoms) ÷ M_r
= (63.5 × 1) ÷ 79.5 = 0.8
Mass = 0.8 × 500 g = 400 g.
So more metal could be obtained from the copper oxide.

Pages 60-61 — Metals

Q1 a) A, B and D

b) All metals are good conductors of electricity. Element C is not a good conductor of electricity so it can't be a metal.

Q2 a) 3

b) 2

c) 3

Q3 a) giant

b) heat, electricity (in either order)

c) malleable

Module C6 — Chemical Synthesis

Q4 a)

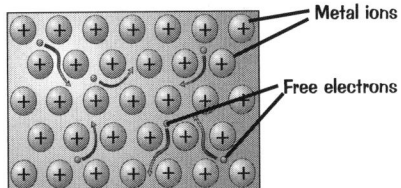

Metal ions

Free electrons

b) The (outer) electrons are free to move through the material.

Q5 a) high
b) strong
c) hammered, malleable

Q6 Metals contain free electrons which can move through the structure and carry the electrical current.

Q7 Metals have high melting points because there is a strong attraction between the free electrons and the closely packed positive ions. Much of this force needs to be overcome in order for the metal to melt, which requires lots of heat.

Page 62 — Environmental Impact

Q1 a) Finite resources are resources that can't be replaced — they could eventually run out.

b) They could run out and if they do, new materials will need to take their place. Recycling metal can help to reduce this problem.

Q2 Any two from each:
Social factors: e.g. new jobs available for locals / improved local transport services / influx of people might put strain on local services.
Economic factors: e.g. more money in local economy / more jobs available / more goods made from the extracted metal are available.
Environmental factors: e.g. pollution such as dust and noise / habitat destruction / scarring of the landscape / deep mine shafts are dangerous if the mine is abandoned / after extraction the area may be turned into a conservation area.

Q3 a) E.g. Deforestation may be required to set up the mines. The mining itself can cause pollution and ruin the landscape.

b) E.g. Producing electricity using fossil fuels means adding to atmospheric CO_2 levels.

c) E.g. More aluminium has to be extracted from bauxite, destroying more rainforest and producing more CO_2. The waste cans would also increase the amount of landfill.

Page 63 — Mixed Questions — Module C5

Q1 a) They have weak forces of attraction between their molecules.

b) They have a giant structure with strong covalent bonds between all of the atoms.

Q2 a) $CaCO_3$
b) i) A white precipitate would form.
ii) $Ca^{2+}(aq) + 2OH^-(aq) \rightarrow$ **$Ca(OH)_2(s)$**
iii) Mixture would fizz / give off bubbles of CO_2.

Q3 a) Aluminium is more reactive than carbon so it cannot be extracted using carbon.

b) $2Al_2O_3(l) \rightarrow 4Al(l) + 3O_2(g)$

c) A_r of Al = 27
M_r of Al_2O_3 = $(2 \times 27) + (3 \times 16)$ = 102
proportion of aluminium in aluminium oxide
$= (A_r \times$ number of atoms$) \div M_r$
$= (27 \times 2) \div 102 = 0.529$
Mass = 0.529×600 g = 317.6 g

d) E.g. it's strong and malleable.

Module C6 — Chemical Synthesis

Page 64 — Industrial Chemical Synthesis

Q1 Chemical synthesis is the process of making complex chemical compounds from simpler ones.

Q2 a) small scale
b) large scale
c) large scale

Q3 a) Making fertilisers.
b) $100 - 35 - 22 - 20 - 6 - 5 - 3 = 9\%$

Q4 a) pharmaceuticals
b) 60 000 people

Pages 65-66 — Acids and Alkalis

Q1 a) neutral
b) 7
c) dyes (or indicators)
d) greater (or higher)
e) blue

Q2 a) distilled water — pale green — 7 — neutral
b) rainwater — yellow — 5/6 — weak acid
c) caustic soda — purple — 14 — strong alkali
d) washing-up liquid — dark green/blue — 8/9 — weak alkali
e) car battery acid — red — 1 — strong acid

Q3 a) less, tartaric, solids, liquid, ethanoic/nitric, nitric/ethanoic, hydrogen chloride
b) E.g. sodium hydroxide, potassium hydroxide, calcium hydroxide.

Q4 a) acid + alkali $\rightarrow$ salt + water
b) i) aqueous hydrogen ions, H+(aq)
ii) aqueous hydroxide ions, OH–(aq)
c) i)

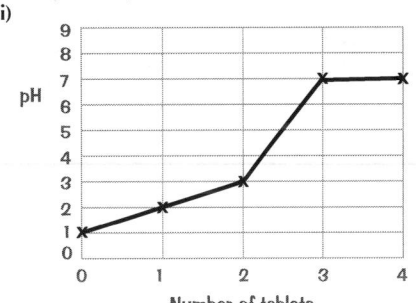

pH

Number of tablets

ii) 3
d) E.g. using an indicator such as universal indicator / using a pH meter.

Q5 a) The hydrogen ions from the acid react with the hydroxide ions from the alkali to make water.
b) $H^+ + OH^- \rightarrow H_2O$

Page 67 — Acids Reacting with Metals

Q1 a)

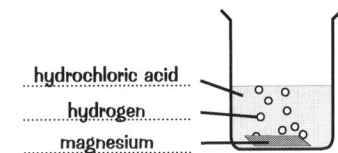

hydrochloric acid
hydrogen
magnesium

b) magnesium + **hydrochloric acid** $\rightarrow$ magnesium chloride + **hydrogen**
c) $Mg(s) + 2HCl(aq) \rightarrow MgCl_2(aq) + H_2(g)$
d) zinc + sulfuric acid $\rightarrow$ zinc sulfate + hydrogen

Q2 a) $Ca(s) + 2HCl(aq) \rightarrow CaCl_2(aq) + H_2(g)$
b) $Zn(s) + 2HCl(aq) \rightarrow ZnCl_2(aq) + H_2(g)$
c) $Mg(s) + H_2SO_4(aq) \rightarrow MgSO_4(aq) + H_2(g)$
d) i) $Mg(s) + \mathbf{2}HBr(aq) \rightarrow MgBr_2(aq) + H_2(g)$
ii) $2Al(s) + 6HBr(aq) \rightarrow 2AlBr_3(aq) + 3H_2(g)$

Module C6 — Chemical Synthesis

Pages 68-69 — Oxides, Hydroxides and Carbonates

Q1 a) acid + metal oxide $\rightarrow$ salt + water
b) acid + metal carbonate $\rightarrow$ salt + water + carbon dioxide
c) acid + metal hydroxide $\rightarrow$ salt + water

Q2 a) hydrochloric acid + lead oxide $\rightarrow$ **lead** chloride + water.
b) nitric acid + copper hydroxide $\rightarrow$ copper **nitrate** + water.
c) sulfuric acid + zinc oxide $\rightarrow$ zinc sulfate + **water**
d) hydrochloric acid + **sodium** oxide $\rightarrow$ sodium **chloride** + **water**
e) **nitric** acid + copper oxide $\rightarrow$ **copper** nitrate + **water**
f) nitric acid + **sodium** hydroxide $\rightarrow$ sodium **nitrate** + **water**

Q3 a) $2HNO_3(aq) + Na_2CO_3(s) \rightarrow 2NaNO_3(aq) + H_2O(l) + CO_2(g)$
b) $H_2SO_4(aq) + MgCO_3(s) \rightarrow MgSO_4(aq) + H_2O(l) + CO_2(g)$

Q4 a) $H_2SO_4(aq) + CuO(s) \rightarrow CuSO_4(aq) + H_2O(l)$
b) $2HNO_3(aq) + MgO(s) \rightarrow Mg(NO_3)_2(aq) + H_2O(l)$
c) $H_2SO_4(aq) + 2NaOH(aq) \rightarrow Na_2SO_4(aq) + 2H_2O(l)$

Q5 a) $H_2SO_4(aq) + CaCO_3(s) \rightarrow CaSO_4(aq) + H_2O(l) + CO_2(g)$
b) $2HNO_3(aq) + MgCO_3(s) \rightarrow Mg(NO_3)_2(aq) + H_2O(l) + CO_2(g)$
c) $2HCl(aq) + K_2CO_3(s) \rightarrow 2KCl(aq) + H_2O(l) + CO_2(g)$
d) $2HCl(aq) + CaCO_3(s) \rightarrow CaCl_2(aq) + H_2O(l) + CO_2(g)$
e) $H_2SO_4(aq) + Na_2CO_3(s) \rightarrow Na_2SO_4(aq) + H_2O(l) + CO_2(g)$

Q6 a) i) Carbon dioxide gas is produced in the reaction.
ii) Hydrochloric acid + copper carbonate $\rightarrow$ copper chloride + water + carbon dioxide
b) copper carbonate
c) $2HCl + Cu(OH)_2 \rightarrow CuCl_2 + 2H_2O$

Pages 70-71 — Synthesising Compounds

Q1 an acid and an alkali react to produce a salt — neutralisation
a compound breaks down on heating — thermal decomposition
an insoluble solid forms when two solutions are mixed — precipitation

Q2 a) injury, hazards, harmed, action, reduce
b) E.g. accurately calculating the amounts of reactants will help reduce the amount of waste produced, which will help increase profits.
c) E.g. the amount of product and reactants / whether the reaction is explosive/gives out heat etc.
d) E.g. temperature / concentration/pressure

Q3 a) E.g. to purify the product.
b) E.g. To isolate a product that is dissolved in the reaction mixture/solvent.
c) E.g. To remove any excess water from the product.

Q4 a) i) neutralisation
ii) $NaOH(aq) + HBr(aq) \rightarrow NaBr(aq) + H_2O(l)$
b) E.g. filtration
c) The yield is calculated to give an indication of the overall success of the process.
d) E.g. crystallisation

Pages 72-73 — Calculating Masses in Reactions

Q1 a) $2Mg + O_2 \rightarrow 2MgO$
b)

$2Mg$	$2MgO$
$2 \times 24 = 48$	$2 \times (24 + 16) = 80$
Divide by 48 g to get 1 g.	
$48 \div 48 = 1$ g	$80 \div 48 = 1.67$ g
$1 \times 10 = 10$ g	$1.67 \times 10 = \mathbf{16.7\ g}$

Q2

$4Na$	$2Na_2O$
$4 \times 23 = 92$	$2 \times [(2 \times 23) + 16] = 124$
Divide by 124 g to get 1 g.	
$92 \div 124 = 0.74$ g	$124 \div 124 = 1$ g
$0.74 \times 2 = \mathbf{1.48\ g}$	$1 \times 2 = 2$ g

Q3 a) $2Al + Fe_2O_3 \rightarrow Al_2O_3 + 2Fe$
b)

Fe_2O_3	$2Fe$
$[(2 \times 56) + (3 \times 16)] = 160$	$2 \times 56 = 112$
Divide by 160 g to get 1 g.	
$160 \div 160 = 1$ g	$112 \div 160 = 0.7$
$1 \times 20 = 20$ g	$0.7 \times 20 = \mathbf{14\ g}$

Q4 $CaCO_3 \rightarrow CaO + CO_2$

$CaCO_3$	CaO
$40 + 12 + (3 \times 16) = 100$	$40 + 16 = 56$
Divide by 56 kg to get 1 kg.	
$100 \div 56 = 1.786$ kg	$56 \div 56 = 1$ kg
$1.786 \times 100 = \mathbf{178.6\ kg}$	$1 \times 100 = 100$ kg

Q5

C	$2CO$
12	$2 \times (12 + 16) = 56$
Divide by 12 g to get 1 g.	
$12 \div 12 = 1$ g	$56 \div 12 = 4.67$ g
$1 \times 10 = 10$ g	$4.67 \times 10 = 46.7$ g

46.7 g of CO is produced in stage B — all of this is used in stage C.

CO	CO_2
$12 + 16 = 28$	$12 + (2 \times 16) = 44$
Divide by 28 g to get 1 g.	
$28 \div 28 = 1$ g	$44 \div 28 = 1.57$ g
$1 \times 46.7 = 46.7$ g	$1.57 \times 46.7 = \mathbf{73.3\ g}$

Q6 a) $2NaOH + H_2SO_4 \rightarrow Na_2SO_4 + 2H_2O$
b)

$2NaOH$	Na_2SO_4
$2 \times (23 + 16 + 1) = 80$	$(2 \times 23) + 32 + (4 \times 16) = 142$
Divide by 142 g to get 1 g.	
$80 \div 142 = 0.56$ g	$142 \div 142 = 1$ g
$0.56 \times 75 = \mathbf{42.3\ g}$	$1 \times 75 = 75$ g

c)

H_2SO_4	$2H_2O$
$(2 \times 1) + 32 + (4 \times 16) = 98$	$2 \times [(2 \times 1) + 16] = 36$
Divide by 98 g to get 1 g.	
$98 \div 98 = 1$ g	$36 \div 98 = 0.367$ g
$1 \times 50 = 50$ g	$0.367 \times 50 = \mathbf{18.4\ g}$

Page 74 — Purification and Measuring Yield

Q1 a)

This is the mass of pure dry product. It is found by **weighing** the dried product.

$$\text{percentage yield} = \frac{\text{actual yield}}{\text{theoretical yield}} \times 100$$

This is the **actual yield** of the product as a percentage of the **theoretical yield**.

This is the **maximum** amount of **pure**, dried product that could have been made using the amounts of **reactants** you started with.

b) $(1.2 \div 2.7) \times 100 = 44.4\%$
c) filtration
d) E.g. using a drying oven, using a desiccator.

Q2 E.g. heating up the solution will cause the solute to evaporate, leaving behind solid crystals of the product.

Page 75 — Titrations

Q1 a) Titrations can't be carried out using solids, only liquids.
b)

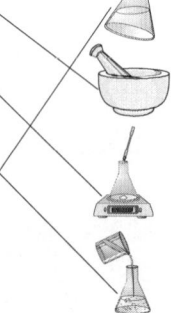

Crush the solid product into a powder.

Weigh some of the powdered product into a titration flask.

The powder is then **dissolved** by adding some **solvent** (e.g. **water**)

Swirl the flask until all of the solid has dissolved.

Module C6 — Chemical Synthesis

c)

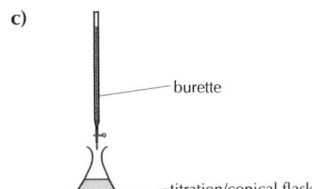

burette

titration/conical flask

d) Add some alkali to a titration/conical flask with a few drops of indicator. Fill a burette with acid. Add some acid to the alkali from the burette, regularly swirling the flask. Record the volume of acid when the indicator changes colour. (Titrations can also be carried out by adding alkali to acid.)

Page 76 — Purity

Q1 a) Any two of, e.g. filtration / evaporation / recrystallisation.
  b) Chemicals which are consumed by humans must be safe. Impurities in drugs could be dangerous.
Q2 a) neutralisation
  b) i) First calculate vol. of NaOH in dm^3:
      $21.6 \div 1000 = 0.0216 \ dm^3$
      Then the vol. of citric acid in dm^3:
      $25 \div 1000 = 0.025 \ dm^3$
      Concentration of citric acid
      $= 4.8 \times [(2.5 \times 0.0216) \div 0.025] = 10.37 \ g/dm^3$
  ii) Mass of citric acid $= 10.37 \times 0.025 = 0.2592 \ g$
  iii) % purity $= 0.2592 \div 0.3 \times 100 = 86.4\%$

Page 77 — Energy Transfer in Reactions

Q1 energy, exothermic, heat, an increase, endothermic, heat, a decrease
Q2 a) A, C and D
  b) B and E
Q3 a) E.g. the reaction gives out heat. This heat must be removed or the reaction may get too hot.
  b) E.g. the reaction needs to be heated otherwise the rate of reaction may slow down too much.

Pages 78-79 — Rates of Reaction

Q1 a) Slow: an apple rotting; a ship rusting
      Moderate speed: hair being dyed
      Fast: a firework exploding; a match burning
  b) E.g. the rate of a chemical reaction is how fast reactants are turned into products.
Q2 safety, fast, explosion, economic, optimum, compromise, yield, costs
Q3 a) Q
  b) R
  c)

Volume of gas produced

R

Q

P

Time (s)

Q4 a) E.g. to increase the rate of the reaction
  b) Any two of e.g. to make the reaction more safe / to lower production costs / to burn less fuel and help protect the environment.
Q5 a) E.g. The volume of acid, the temperature, the size and shape of the magnesium strips.

b)

300

250

200

time (s)

150

100

50

0

0   0.05   0.1   0.15   0.2
concentration (mol/dm³)

c) The more concentrated the acid, the faster the rate of the reaction.
d) Yes. The reaction would be faster with magnesium powder.

Page 80 — Collision Theory

Q1 collide, more often, more energy, rate of reaction
Q2 a) Increase — the particles are closer together so there are more frequent collisions.
  b)

low concentration   high concentration

Q3 a) False
  b) True
  c) False
  d) True
  e) False
Q4 A catalyst is a substance which increases the speed of a chemical reaction without being used up or changed itself.

Page 81 — Measuring Rates of Reaction

Q1 speed, reactants, products
Q2 a) E.g.

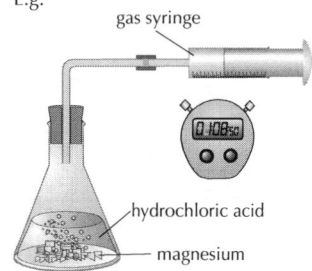

gas syringe

hydrochloric acid

magnesium

b) Place a flask containing the hydrochloric acid and magnesium onto a balance and record the change in mass over time.
Q3 a) precipitation
  b) Place the solution on a piece of paper with a mark drawn on it. Observe how long it takes for the mark to disappear.

Page 82 — Mixed Questions — Module C6

Q1 a) Red
  b) i) $2HCl(aq) + Mg(OH)_2(s) \rightarrow MgCl_2(aq) + 2H_2O(l)$
  ii) neutralisation

Module P4 — Explaining Motion

c) i) The reaction is exothermic, so heat is given out.

ii)

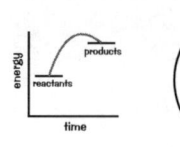 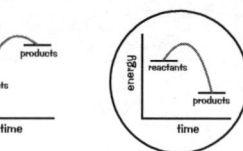

iii) E.g. place the reaction in an ice bath to cool down.

d) i) E.g. evaporation / crystallisation.

ii) E.g. he should dissolve the product and then evaporate the solution again.

iii) $(3.2 \text{ g} \div 4.2 \text{ g}) \times 100 = 76.2\%$

Module P4 — Explaining Motion

Page 83 — Speed

Q1 a) 5 minutes = $5 \times 60 = 300$ s, so
$$\text{speed} = \frac{\text{distance}}{\text{time}} = \frac{1500}{300} = 5 \text{ m/s}$$

b) Rearrange the formula for time —
$$\text{time} = \frac{\text{distance}}{\text{speed}} = \frac{300}{15} = 20 \text{ s}$$

c) Distance = speed × time = $4 \times (8 \times 60) = 1920$ m

Q2 You need to find the total time it would take for each of the takeaways to reach the house.

Ludo's Pizza:
$$\text{Time for delivery} = \frac{\text{distance}}{\text{speed}} = \frac{6.5}{30} = 0.217 \text{ h}$$
Time taken to cook the food is 0.25 hours, so the total time is 0.47 hours.

Moonlight Indian Takeaway:
$$\text{Time for delivery} = \frac{\text{distance}}{\text{speed}} = \frac{4}{40} = 0.1 \text{ h}$$
Time taken to cook the food is 0.5 hours, so the total time is 0.6 hours.
So they should order from Ludo's Pizza.

Q3 a) 50 miles = $50 \times 1609 = 80\,450$ m
1 hour = $60 \times 60 = 3600$ s
$$\text{speed} = \frac{\text{distance}}{\text{time}} = \frac{80\,450}{3600} = 22.3 \text{ m/s}$$
So 50 mph is about 22 m/s.

b) Car moves 3 lots of 2 m (= 6 m) in 0.2 seconds.
$$\text{Therefore speed of car} = \frac{\text{distance}}{\text{time}} = \frac{6}{0.2} = 30 \text{ m/s}.$$
This is above 22 m/s (see **a)**) so the car was breaking the speed limit.

Pages 84-85 — Speed, Distance and Velocity

Q1 a) Distance = speed × time = $10 \times 300 = 3000$ m.

b)

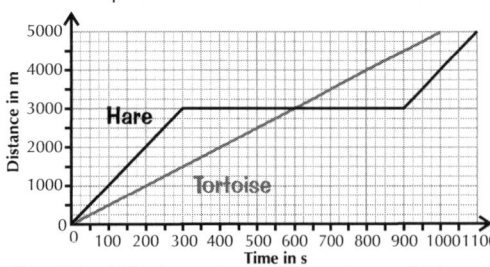

c) After 600 s / 10 minutes (read off from the graph where the two lines cross).

d) The tortoise got to the finish line after 1000 s, and the hare took 1100 s. Therefore the tortoise had to wait for 100 s before the hare reached the finish line.

Q2 The graph shows that the motorist accelerates for about 1.5 seconds, then travels at a constant speed.
The gradient of the graph between 1.5 s and 3.0 s will give you the speed.
Gradient = vertical change ÷ horizontal change = $(72 - 18) \div (3.0 - 1.5) = 54 \div 1.5 = 36$ m/s. This is above 31 m/s so he was exceeding the speed limit.

Q3 a) True

b) False

c) True

d) False

Q4 a) A — acceleration (increasing velocity), B — constant velocity, C — deceleration (decreasing velocity), D — stationary.

b) The distance travelled in section B is 9 m – 3 m = 6 m. The time taken is 6 s – 3 s = 3 s.
$$\text{So, speed} = \frac{\text{distance}}{\text{time}} = \frac{6}{3} = 2 \text{ m/s}.$$

c) E.g.

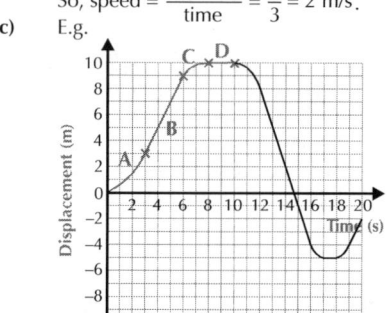

Pages 86-87 — Acceleration and Velocity

Q1 A — (constant) acceleration (from 0 - 3 m/s)
B — constant speed/velocity (of 3 m/s)
C — (constant) acceleration (from 3 - 9 m/s)
D — constant speed/velocity (of 9 m/s)
E — (constant) deceleration (from 9 - 7 m/s)

Q2 Line A = Line 3
Line B = Line 2
Line C = Line 1

Q3 a) Since the egg was dropped from rest, its change in speed is 80 m/s. Putting the numbers into the formula you get
$$\text{acceleration} = \frac{\text{change in velocity}}{\text{time}} = \frac{80}{8} = 10 \text{ m/s}^2.$$

b) Rearrange the formula to get
$$\text{time} = \frac{\text{change in velocity}}{\text{acceleration}} = \frac{40}{10} = 4 \text{ s}.$$

Q4 Rearranging the formula for acceleration you get:
change in speed = acceleration × time = $2 \times 4 = 8$ m/s.
Change in speed = final speed – initial speed, so initial speed = final speed – change in speed = 24 – 8 = 16 m/s.

Q5 a) Acceleration = gradient = $8 \div 5 = 1.6$ m/s^2.

b) See black line below.

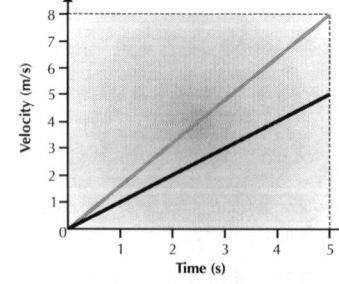

Module P4 — Explaining Motion

Q6 a)

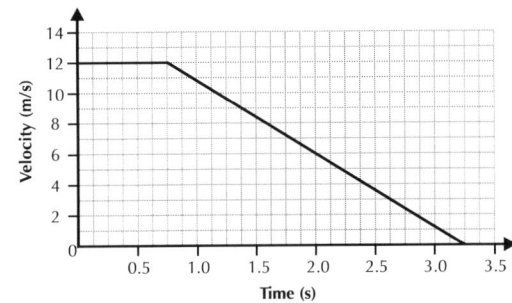

b) Acceleration = $\dfrac{\text{change in velocity}}{\text{time}} = \dfrac{-12}{2.5} = -4.8$ m/s².
So deceleration = 4.8 m/s².

Page 88 — Forces and Friction

Q1 force, interaction, 150, equal, opposite

Q2 a) The surface of the slide and the penguin's back.

b)

friction

c) E.g. By coating the slide and/or himself in some kind of lubricant (e.g. grease). / By reducing the area of his body that touches the slide.

Q3 a)

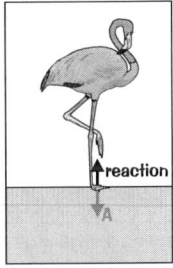

reaction

A

b) Force A is exerted by the **flamingo** on the **ground**. Force B is exerted by the **ground** on the **flamingo**.

Q4 a) The exhaust gases accelerate because the **jet engine** exerts **a force** on them.

b) The jet exerts a force on the exhaust gases (making them accelerate backwards), so the exhaust gases exert an equal and opposite force on the jet, making it move forwards.

Page 89 — Forces

Q1 a) The teapot's weight is balanced by a reaction force from the table.

b) Gravity / its weight acting downwards and a tension/reaction force from the rope acting upwards.

c) The forces should be drawn as arrows of the same size but in opposite directions. E.g.

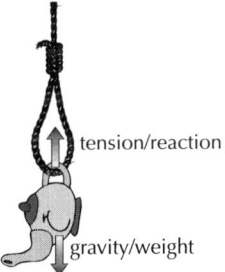

tension/reaction

gravity/weight

Q2 Statement D should be circled.

Q3 a)

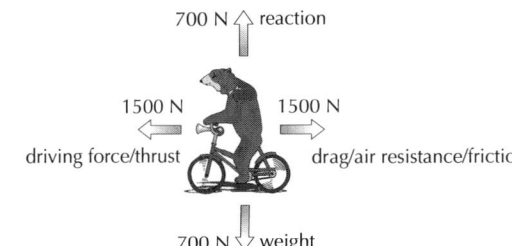

700 N ⤒ reaction

1500 N ⇦   ⇨ 1500 N

driving force/thrust   drag/air resistance/friction

700 N ⤓ weight

b) backwards/to the right of the page

Page 90 — Forces and Momentum

Q1 a) 1 500 000 – 1 500 000 = 0 N

b) 6 000 000 – 1 500 000 = 4 500 000 N

Q2 X = unbalanced force of gravity. You can tell this because the graph is curved, so there must be an acceleration.
Y = forces in balance. You can tell this because the graph here is a straight line so the object must be falling at a constant speed — there is no acceleration.
Z = reaction force from ground acts. You can tell this because at Z the gradient of the line changes abruptly and becomes negative, showing that the ball has changed direction (accelerated) — this was when it hit the ground.

Q3 Momentum = mass × velocity
Truck A's momentum = 3000 kg × 30 m/s = 90 000 kg m/s.
Truck B's momentum = 4500 kg × 10 m/s = 45 000 kg m/s.
Truck C's momentum = 4000 kg × 20 m/s = 80 000 kg m/s.
Truck D's momentum = 3500 kg × 15 m/s = 52 500 kg m/s.
So the order of increasing momentum is: B, D, C, A.

Page 91 — Change in Momentum and Force

Q1 a) Change in momentum = resultant force × time
= 8000 × 1.9 = 15 200 kg m/s.

b) If the time period was shorter for the same change in momentum, the resultant force must have been larger than 8000 N.

Q2 a) A crumple zone crumples on impact, increasing the time taken for the car to change momentum and stop, which decreases the forces acting on the people inside the car.

b) E.g. seat belts, air bags.

Q3 a) Momentum of car = mass × velocity
= 1200 kg × 30 m/s = 36 000 kg m/s.

b) When the car has stopped its momentum = 0 kg m/s.
So the change in momentum is 36 000 kg m/s.
Average force = Change in momentum ÷ time
= 36 000 kg m/s ÷ 1.2 s = 30 000 N.

c) In a collision, the seat belts will stretch and reduce the forces on the passengers by increasing the time taken for them to stop moving. (It also prevents the passengers from hitting hard objects inside the car, e.g. the steering wheel.)

Page 92 — Work

Q1 a) Work involves the transfer of **energy**.

b) To do work a **force** acts over a **distance**.

c) Work is measured in **joules**.

Q2 a) True

b) True

c) False

d) True

Q3 a) Work done = force × distance = 1200 N × 8 m = 9600 J.

b) Kinetic energy (the donkey is moving), heat energy (because of friction between the donkey's feet and the surface of the track) and some sound energy.

Q4 a) gravity / his weight

b) Work done = force × distance moved
= 600 N × (10 × 0.2) m = 1200 J.

Module P5 — Electric Circuits

c) 15 kJ = 15 000 J
Distance = work done ÷ force = 15 000 J ÷ 600 N = 25 m.
Each step is 0.2 m high, so the number of rungs Ben must climb is 25 ÷ 0.2 = 125 rungs.

Page 93 — Kinetic Energy

Q1 K.E. = $\frac{1}{2}mv^2$ = $\frac{1}{2}$ × 200 × (9)^2 = 0.5 × 200 × 81 = 8100 J

Q2 9 J = $\frac{1}{2}$ × m × (20)^2 = $\frac{1}{2}$ × m × 400 = 200 × m
so, m = 9 ÷ 200 = 0.045 kg

Q3 90 750 J = $\frac{1}{2}$ × 60 × v^2 = 30 × v^2
so, v = $\sqrt{(90\ 750 ÷ 30)}$ = $\sqrt{3025}$ = 55 m/s

Q4 a) i) 614 400 J = $\frac{1}{2}$ × 1200 × v^2 = 600 × v^2
so, v = $\sqrt{(614\ 400 ÷ 600)}$ = $\sqrt{1024}$ = 32 m/s

   ii) 614 400 J = $\frac{1}{2}$ × 12 288 × v^2 = 6144 × v^2
so, v = $\sqrt{(614\ 400 ÷ 6144)}$ = $\sqrt{100}$ = 10 m/s

b) The car has more kinetic energy — doubling speed increases K.E. by a factor of 2^2 = 4, whereas trebling mass only increases K.E. by a factor of 3.

Q5 a) The pushing force does work on the bicycle so increases its kinetic energy and velocity.

b) Assume that air resistance and friction can be ignored, because this means Jack's kinetic energy will increase by the same amount as the work done. (His change in velocity can then be calculated from the change in kinetic energy.)

Pages 94-95 — Gravitational Potential Energy

Q1 a) G.P.E. = weight × vertical height = 250 N × 1.2 m = 300 J

b) Total G.P.E. = 28 × 300 J = 8400 J

c) The energy transferred and the work done by Fred are the same thing, so 8400 J.

Q2 a) A — maximum G.P.E.
B — G.P.E. is being converted to K.E.
C — minimum G.P.E., maximum K.E.
D — K.E. is being converted to G.P.E.

b) i) At half the height, half the potential energy should have been converted into kinetic energy, i.e. 300 kJ ÷ 2 = 150 kJ.

   ii) K.E. = $\frac{1}{2}mv^2$
150 000 = $\frac{1}{2}$ × 750 × v^2
150 000 = 375 × v^2
v = $\sqrt{(150\ 000 ÷ 375)}$ = $\sqrt{400}$ = 20 m/s

   iii) Air resistance and friction will cause some of the G.P.E. to be dissipated through heating, so the K.E. and hence the speed, will be lower than the value calculated in part **ii)**. There will also be a little energy wasted as sound too.

Q3 a) Rearrange G.P.E. = weight × height:
$$\text{height} = \frac{\text{G.P.E.}}{\text{weight}} = \frac{4000}{500} = 8 \text{ m}$$

b) The energy converted from potential energy to kinetic energy is 1500 J, so the difference must be the wasted energy. 4000 J – 1500 J = 2500 J.

c) friction/air resistance/drag

Q4 a) Work done = change in energy.
Change in G.P.E. = weight × change in height
= 700 × 20 = 14 000 J

b) The skier converts all of her gravitational potential energy into kinetic energy, so has 14 000 J of kinetic energy.

c) K.E. = $\frac{1}{2}$ × m × v^2
14 000 = $\frac{1}{2}$ × 70 × v^2
14 000 = 35 × v^2
v = $\sqrt{(14\ 000 ÷ 35)}$ = $\sqrt{400}$ = 20 m/s

Q5 a) Just before the ball hits the ground, it has converted all of its gravitational potential energy into kinetic energy, so it has 121 J of kinetic energy.

b) K.E. = $\frac{1}{2}$ × m × v^2
121 = $\frac{1}{2}$ × 0.1 × v^2
121 = 0.05 × v^2
v = $\sqrt{(121 ÷ 0.05)}$ = $\sqrt{242}$ = 49.2 m/s

Pages 96-97 — Mixed Questions — Module P4

Q1 a) Work done = force × distance = 300 × 1500
= 450 000 J (or 450 kJ).

b) Acceleration = change in speed ÷ time taken
= 20 ÷ 6.2 = 3.23 m/s^2.

c) Momentum = mass × velocity
= 1200 × 20 = 24 000 kg m/s
Change in momentum = force × time
So, force = change in momentum ÷ time
= 24 000 ÷ 0.8 = 30 000 N.

d) His seat belt would have stretched slightly, increasing the time taken to change his momentum, so he would have experienced a smaller force.

Q2 a) G.P.E. = weight × height = 12 000 × 34
= 408 000 J (= 408 kJ).

b) Two thirds of the potential energy is converted into kinetic energy, so gain in K.E. = 408 000 × 2/3 = 272 000 J.
So, two thirds of the way down:
K.E. = $\frac{1}{2}mv^2$
272 000 = $\frac{1}{2}$ × 1200 × v^2
272 000 = 600 × v^2
v = $\sqrt{(272\ 000 ÷ 600)}$ = 21.3 m/s.

c) Time = change in speed ÷ acceleration
= 12 ÷ 6.4 = 1.875 s.

Q3 a) 120 s – 60 s = 60 s (1 minute).

b) Both lines are straight (initially).

c) Train 1 is faster, because the gradient is steeper.
Speed = gradient = 50 m ÷ 40 s = 1.25 m/s.

d) Train 1 is decelerating/has a negative acceleration/is slowing down.

Q4 a) As soon as it's dropped the dummy accelerates under the influence of gravity. So as it falls its velocity increases steadily. When it hits the ground its velocity changes almost instantly to zero and stays at zero.

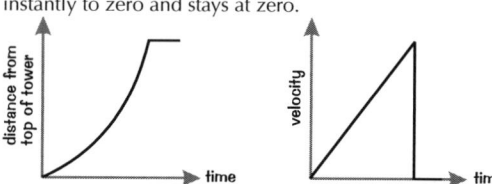

b) Yes — its weight and the reaction force from the ground.

c) i) Work done = potential energy gained
= weight × height = 950 × 60 = 57 000 J (or 57 kJ).

   ii) Speed = distance ÷ time
time = distance ÷ speed = 60 m ÷ 0.8 m/s = 75 s.

Module P5 — Electric Circuits

Page 98 — Static Electricity

Q1 static, insulating, friction, electrons, positive/negative, negative/positive

Q2 Circled: positive and negative, negative and positive
Underlined: positive and positive, negative and negative

Q3 a) True

b) False

c) False

Q4 Lisa: static electricity can build up when you brush your hair giving each strand the same charge, so they repel each other. The opposite charge builds up on the brush, so the hair is attracted to the brush.
Sara: when Sara's mum cleans the TV screen she causes a build-up of static electricity on it. Dust particles are attracted to the charged TV screen.
Tim: when Tim takes his jumper off electrons get scraped off one layer of clothing onto another. The 'extra' electrons on one layer of clothing are attracted back to the material they came from, causing small sparks and the crackling sound.

Module P5 — Electric Circuits

Pages 99-100 — Electric Current

Q1 a) flow, charge
b) voltage, force
c) resistance
Q2 A — Current — amperes
V — Voltage — volts
Ω — Resistance — ohms
Q3 a) False
b) True
c) True
d) False
Q4 a) The wires in an electrical circuit are full of charges that are free to move.
b) battery / cell / power supply
c) components / resistance
d) Increasing the voltage of the power supply.
Q5 Ranjit
Q6 transferred, charge, rate, energy
Q7 a) Increasing the voltage of the battery increases the current.
b) i) By decreasing resistance.
ii) By increasing resistance.
Q8

	Player A	Player B	Player C
Voltage (V)	12	**3**	230
Current (A)	2.5	40	**2**
Power (W)	**30**	120	460

Page 101 — Electric Circuits

Q1 Cell — Provides the 'push' on the charge.

Variable Resistor — Used to alter the current.

Component — The item you're testing.

Voltmeter — Measures the voltage.

Ammeter — Measures the current.

Q2 a) 1. battery
2. thermistor
3. fixed resistor
4. LDR
5. switch (closed)
6. filament lamp
b) The ammeter must be drawn in series between the battery and the first junction — see diagram for answer **c)**.
c) The voltmeter must be drawn in parallel around the lamp — see below.

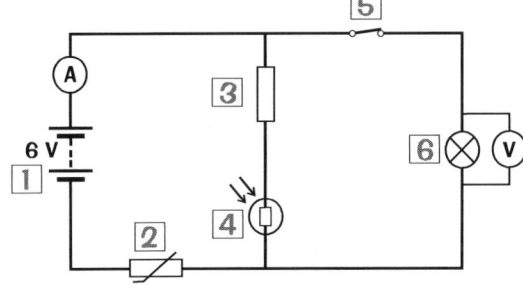

Q3 potential difference, energy, charge, battery, energy, components, parallel

Pages 102-103 — Resistance

Q1 a) D
b) E.g. D has the shallowest/least steep gradient.
c) Resistance = voltage ÷ current (for any point on the line)
= 2 ÷ 4 = 0.5 Ω
Q2 a) False
b) False

c) True
d) False
Q3

Voltage (V)	Current (A)	Resistance (Ω)
6	2	**3**
8	**4**	2
9	3	3
4	8	**0.5**
2	**0.5**	4
1	0.5	2

Q4 a) Collisions between the moving charges and stationary ions in the filament wire cause the ions to vibrate faster, increasing the temperature.
b) So that they get so hot that they glow and give out light.
Q5 a) i) The resistance of the wires is assumed to be zero/negligible.
ii) The resistance of connecting wires is usually very small.
b) He could work out the resistance for each pair of readings using R = V ÷ I, then calculate an average. / He could plot a graph of V against I and use the gradient to calculate R.
Q6 a) The graph must be a straight line through the origin, e.g.

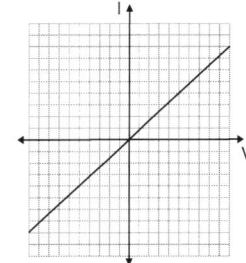

b) i) It decreased its resistance.
ii) An LDR.
c) i) A thermistor.
ii) The resistance will gradually decrease as the temperature increases.

Page 104 — Series Circuits

Q1 Same everywhere in the circuit — Current
Shared by all the components — Total potential difference
The sum of the resistances — Total resistance
Can be different for each component — Potential difference
Q2 a) A battery/cell.
b) i) The lamp (with voltage V_3).
ii) E.g. The most work is done by the charge passing through the lamp and the least passing through resistor R_1.
c) Because the battery has to push charge through all of the components. / Because the total resistance is the sum of the individual resistances.
Q3 a) i) 0.2 A
ii) The current is the same everywhere in a series circuit.
b) i) V_1
ii) Voltage is a measure of how much work is done on or by the charge. The work done on each unit of charge is the same in both circuits because the battery voltage is the same. But in circuit 2 the charge needs to do work to pass through two lamps instead of one, so there will be less work done on each lamp than in circuit 1. So the voltage across each lamp will be lower in circuit 2.

Page 105 — Parallel Circuits

Q1 a) True
b) True
c) True
Q2 a) No change because all components in a parallel circuit get the full source potential difference.

Module P5 — Electric Circuits

b) No change because the current through each component is the same as if it were the only component in the circuit.

c) No change, because the resistance of a component is fixed.

Q3 a) i) $0.27 + 0.43 = 0.7$ A

ii) The currents flowing through each branch of a parallel circuit must add up to the total current leaving the battery/cell.

b) i) More current flows through resistor R_2 than R_1, so R_2 must have the smallest resistance.

ii) Smaller because the branches of the circuit provide more paths for the charges to flow along.

c) 0.27 A (The current through R_1 will stay the same.)

Pages 106-107 — Mains Electricity

Q1 a) 230 V

b) Batteries supply direct current, mains electricity uses alternating current.

c) electromagnetic induction

Q2 voltage, moving, electromagnetic, induction, magnet, coil, alternating, complete

Q3 a) i) negative

ii) negative

b) i) Nothing — voltage is only induced when there is a changing magnetic field.

ii) The voltage induced will keep swapping from positive to negative as the magnet changes direction. / An alternating voltage will be induced.

Q4 a) i) Its direction reverses.

ii) Its direction reverses.

b) AC

c) AC is easier to generate and can be distributed more easily/efficiently over long distances than DC.

Q5 A

Q6 a) AC voltage is induced because the coil experiences a magnetic field which is varying in direction.

b) The induced voltage would be in the opposite direction (when the magnet is at any given position).

c) Any three from: Increase the speed of the hamster (increase the speed of rotation). / Increase the strength of the magnetic field. / Increase the number of turns in the coil. / Put the coil around an iron core.

Page 108 — Transformers

Q1 1. An alternating voltage is connected to the primary coil of a transformer.
2. An alternating current flows in the primary coil.
3. This causes a rapidly-changing magnetic field in the core.
4. The changing magnetic field induces an alternating voltage in the secondary coil.
5. An alternating current can flow in a circuit connected to the secondary coil.

Q2 a) A transformer consists of two coils of wire wound on an iron core.

b) A step-up transformer induces a larger voltage in the secondary coil than in the primary coil, while a step-down transformer induces a smaller voltage.

c) The magnetic field created in the core must be constantly changing in order to induce a voltage in the secondary coil.

Q3

Number of turns on primary coil	Voltage to primary coil (V)	Number of turns on secondary coil	Voltage to secondary coil (V)
1000	12	4000	**48**
1000	**10**	2000	20
1000	12	**1000**	12
71 739	33 000	500	230

Page 109 — Magnetic Fields

Q1 a)

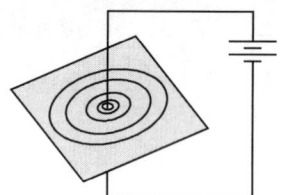

b) The circular magnetic fields around opposite sides of the loop reinforce each other in the centre.
E.g.

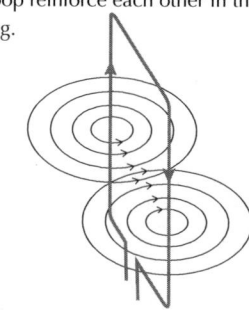

Q2 a) True

b) False. E.g. As more turns are added to a coil its magnetic field gets stronger.

c) False. E.g. A wire that's parallel to the lines of force of a magnetic field feels no force at all.

Q3 a) The wire will move out of the paper (towards the reader).

b) By reversing the direction of the current. / By turning the magnets the other way round (reversing the magnetic field).

c) The magnetic fields of the permanent magnets and the current-carrying wire interact — producing a force.

Page 110 — The Motor Effect

Q1 B

Q2 The split-ring commutator reverses the direction of the current every half turn by swapping the contacts to the DC supply.
A split-ring commutator keeps a motor spinning in the same direction.

Q3 a)

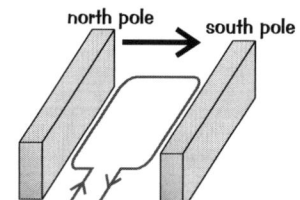

b) Downwards (by using Fleming's Left-Hand Rule).

c) Anticlockwise (left side down, right side up).

d) i) clockwise

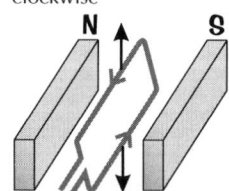

ii) There is a split-ring commutator which swaps the contacts each time the coil gets to a vertical position (i.e. every half turn). This reverses the direction of the current in the coil — so the 'new' left arm has current flowing in the same direction as the 'old' left arm and the motion is the same as before.

e) DVD players contain an electric motor which is connected by an axle to the part of the DVD player that makes the DVD spin.

Module P6 — Radioactive Materials

Pages 111-112 — Mixed Questions
— Module P5

Q1 a) The resistance varies as the switch is turned. The greater the resistance, the less current will flow, so the dimmer the lights will be.

b)

Position	Resistance (Ω)	Current (A)
1	50	**4.6**
2	**100**	2.3
3	**25**	9.2

c) 3

Q2 a) E.g. As she walks across the nylon carpet, electrons are transferred between the carpet and her feet, leaving her charged. When she touches the earthed radiator, she is discharged — and feels the charge flowing through her body to earth.

b) Good electrical conductors have charges (electrons) that are free to move. (Electric current is a flow of charge.)

Q3 a) Total voltage = $12 = V_{lamp} + V_{resistor} + V_{resistor}$
Both resistors have same resistance, so also have the same voltage, so $12 = 4 + (2 \times V_{resistor})$ and so $V_{resistor} = 4\,V$.
The lamp uses the same voltage as a 5 Ω resistor, so the lamp must also have a resistance of 5 Ω

b) Total resistance = $R_{lamp} + R_{resistor} + R_{resistor}$
$= 5 + 5 + 5 = 15\,\Omega$.

c) $R = V \div I$, so $I = V \div R$
$I = 12 \div 15 = 0.8\,A$

d) $P = V \times I$
$P = 4 \times 0.8 = 3.2\,W$

Q4 a) i) $4 \times 0.5 = 2.0\,A$
ii) 0 A (there is not a complete circuit unless switch A is closed).
iii) $(4 \times 0.5) + (2 \times 6.0) = 14.0\,A$

b) There will be 12 V across the de-mister because components connected in parallel all have the same voltage across them.

c) i) A thermistor.
ii) As the temperature falls its resistance increases.

d) i) The motion tells you which way the forces must be acting — see below.

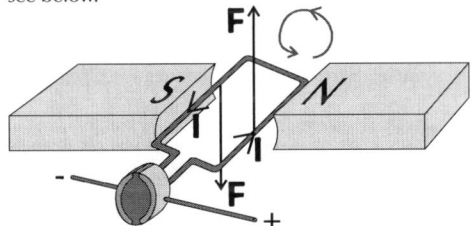

ii) (See diagram above.)
Use Fleming's Left-Hand Rule on one side of the coil.
E.g. for the right-hand side of the coil, the field (first finger) goes from right to left (north to south), the motion (thumb) goes upwards, giving you the current (second finger) going into the page.
iii) (See diagram above.) Once you know which way the current is flowing around the coil, work your way back to the connections at the split-ring.

Module P6 — Radioactive Materials

Page 113 — Radioactivity

Q1

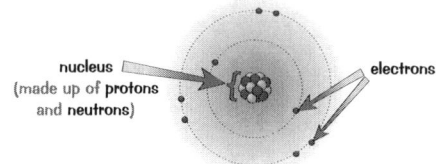

nucleus (made up of protons and neutrons)   electrons

Q2 The following statements should be underlined:
Ionising radiation can transfer enough energy to break molecules apart. Unstable atoms can emit three types of ionising radiation.

Q3 Radioactive atoms are... unstable and decay to become stable.
Unstable atoms decay... at random and unpredictably.
The decay is spontaneous... and not affected by physical conditions.
When atoms decay... they give out radiation.

Q4 a) They will contain different numbers of neutrons.
b) Atoms with the same number of protons but a different number of neutrons.
c) An isotope that is not radioactive.

Pages 114-115 — Radiation

Q1 a) alpha, beta and gamma
b) the nucleus
c) Gamma (it's a form of electromagnetic radiation).
Q2 a) beta and gamma
b) gamma
c) beta and alpha
Q3 big/heavy, heavy/big, slowly, easily, penetrate, heavy/big, protons, two, element, protons
Q4 a) i) $92 - 2 = 90$
ii) $238 - 4 = 234$
b) Thorium (Th)
Q5 Beta particles are made when... a neutron turns into a proton.
An element that loses a... beta particle becomes a new element.
Beta particles come from... nuclei with too many neutrons to be stable.
Beta particles penetrate... moderately into materials.
Beta particles are... quite small and fast.
Q6 a) E.g. any two from: gamma rays have no mass / they are EM waves / they can pass through thin metal sheets / unlike alpha and beta emission, gamma emission doesn't change the atom into a new element.
b) After it has emitted an alpha or beta particle and needs to lose some excess energy.
c) Gamma radiation can penetrate most materials.
d) Gamma rays are just energy. Atoms which emit them neither lose nor gain a proton.

Page 116 — Half-Life

Q1 a) False
b) True
Q2 a) half, decay
b) slowly
c) quickly, short
Q3 a) Half of its radioactive nuclei will have decayed.
b) 125 (87 years is 3 half-lives.)
Q4 After 1 half-life: 720 Bq
After 2 half-lives: 360 Bq
After 3 half-lives: 180 Bq
After 4 half-lives: 90 Bq
After 5 half-lives: 45 Bq
Therefore 5 hours is 5 half-lives.
So 1 half-life = 1 hour.
Q5 a) $24 \div 2 = 12.\ 12 \div 2 = 6.\ 6 \div 2 = 3$.
So 3 half-lives.
$3 \times 5400 = 16\,200$ years
b) $24 \times 2 = 48.\ 48 \times 2 = 96.$ So 2 half-lives.
$2 \times 5400 = 10\,800$ years ago

Page 117 — The Atom and Nuclear Fusion

Q1 a) Alpha particles were fired at gold foil. Most passed straight through, but a small number were deflected back.
b) positively, nucleus, mass, negatively, empty space
Q2 positive, electrostatic, strong, fusion, mass, light

Module P6 — Radioactive Materials

Q3 a) The majority of the alpha particles went straight through the foil, undeflected. So most of the mass must be at the centre and the rest empty space.

b) Alpha particles are positive, so they wouldn't be repelled unless the nucleus was also positive.

Q4 The strong force has a very short range, so as the proton moves away, the strength of the strong force drops very quickly.

Pages 118-119 — Nuclear Fission and Nuclear Power

Q1 uranium, split, fission, uranium, nuclei, equal, neutrons

Q2 a) True
b) True
c) False
d) True
e) False
f) False

Q3 Control rods are used to... absorb some neutrons.
Coolants such as water and CO_2... are used to carry away the heat.
In nuclear reactors... a chain reaction is set up.
A neutron splits a uranium... nucleus releasing more neutrons.
The neutrons released go on... to split more nuclei, releasing more neutrons.
The chain reaction has to be... controlled to prevent overheating.

Q4 a) low
b) high
c) intermediate
d) Intermediate
e) High
f) Low

Q5 a) The site must not be liable to earthquakes or other tectonic activity — this would increase the risk of containers being damaged and waste leaking out.
b) E.g. People who live nearby often object.
c) On site at nuclear power stations.
d) E.g. We may find out more about the dangers of radiation and ways of storing radioactive waste. If the stockpile of waste gets too large, we may need to relax the rules.
e) The half-life of the nuclei in some types of radioactive waste is thousands of years.

Pages 120-121 — Danger from Radiation

Q1 ionising, break, ions, kill, sickness, cancer.

Q2 a) Irradiation does not involve contact with the source. Contamination involves some of the source becoming attached to you (so you continue to be irradiated).
b) i) E.g. drinking/eating something contaminated with a radioactive source / inhaling radioactive dust or gas (e.g. radon) / picking up a radioactive sample.
ii) E.g. flying in a plane at high altitude / working in a nuclear power plant / mining / receiving/performing an X-ray.

Q3 a) E.g. any three from: radiographers / uranium processors / miners / nuclear power station workers / airline staff.
b) E.g. Radiographers — taking X-rays.
Uranium processors — radiation emitted by uranium.
Miners — naturally radioactive rocks.
Nuclear power station workers — radiation emitted by nuclear fuel or waste.
Airline staff — cosmic rays.

Q4 The ions produced by irradiation are very chemically reactive and can move around the body, causing damage as they go.

Q5 a) Background radiation.
b) i) E.g. The radiation dose from an X-ray is 100 times less than the average yearly dose from natural radiation. So the benefits of having an X-ray outweigh the risks from the very small amount of radiation exposure.
ii) Double natural dose = $2 \times 0.002 = 0.004$. One flight = 0.00001, so $0.004 \div 0.00001 = 400$ flights.
iii) Yes. $(1000 \times 0.00001) + 0.008 = 0.018$.

Page 122 — Using Ionising Radiation

Q1 Background radiation is... radiation that is all around us.
Natural radioactive materials... include soil, rocks and the air.
Cosmic rays... come mainly from the Sun.

Q2 $24 \div 2 = 12$. $12 \div 2 = 6$. So two half-lives.
$2 \times 5 = 10$ years

Q3 a) Because it is important to minimise the number of healthy cells that are irradiated.
b) Because large numbers of healthy cells are still killed unavoidably.

Q4 a) So it does not have to be replaced too often.
b) E.g. food.

Q5 Technetium-99m. It has a short half-life so the patient isn't exposed to radiation for very long, and it emits gamma radiation which can escape from the body and be detected.

Pages 123-124 — Mixed Questions — Module P6

Q1 a) E.g. Tracers are radioactive molecules that can be injected or swallowed and their progress around the body followed using an external detector.
b) Alpha radiation is highly ionising in a local area. It can't escape out of the body, so it couldn't be detected by the monitoring equipment.
c) $^{131}_{53}\text{I} \rightarrow {}^{131}_{54}\text{Xe} + {}^{0}_{-1}\text{e}$

Q2 a) nuclear fission
b) A neutron splits a uranium nucleus into two smaller nuclei, releasing energy and more neutrons. These neutrons can then go on to split more nuclei and release more neutrons, and so on.
c) Two nuclei combine (fuse) to create a larger nucleus, releasing energy when they do.

Q3 a) E.g. natural radioactive elements (e.g. in rocks and the air) / space (cosmic rays).
b) Low-level waste — Buried in secure landfill sites.
High-level waste — Sealed in glass and steel then left to cool.
Intermediate-level waste — Sealed in concrete blocks and steel canisters.

Q4 a) Any value from 12.6 to 13.4 hours. (The exact value is 12.7 hours.)
b) Thin aluminium will block beta radiation.
Thick lead will block gamma radiation.
c) It can damage cells without killing them (which can cause cancer). It can also kill cells (which causes radiation sickness or death).

Q5 a) The proportion of C-14 halves every 5730 years. So: 5730 years after death the proportion of C-14 is one in 20 000 000 carbon atoms. 11 460 years after death the proportion is one in 40 000 000. So the bone is 11 460 years old.
b) Isotopes are atoms with the same number of protons but different numbers of neutrons
c) E.g. Sterilising food.

ISBN 978 1 84762 749 0

9 781847 627490

S1HA44